Grandchild
of mine

by Elizabeth Reagan Milo
illustrations by Kyzandrha Zarate

Grandchild of Mine

Elizabeth Reagan Milo
Illustrations by Kyzandrha Zarate
Copyright © 2016 Elizabeth Reagan Milo
All rights reserved.

ISBN: 0692763287

ISBN-13: 978-0692763285

For all Grandparents and Grandparents-to-be
And bonds that know no boundaries,
And love that has no end.

For Poppy and Rita,
who've already met.

You're special!

You're brand new!

There's no one exactly
the same as you!

But there's something familiar
in all of the new.

It's the love that we see,
and feel, and hear in you!

PEEKABOO!

You've got mama's eyes
    and daddy's nose...

I think I recognize
those wriggling toes!

PEEKABOO!

You've got mama's hair
and daddy's chin.

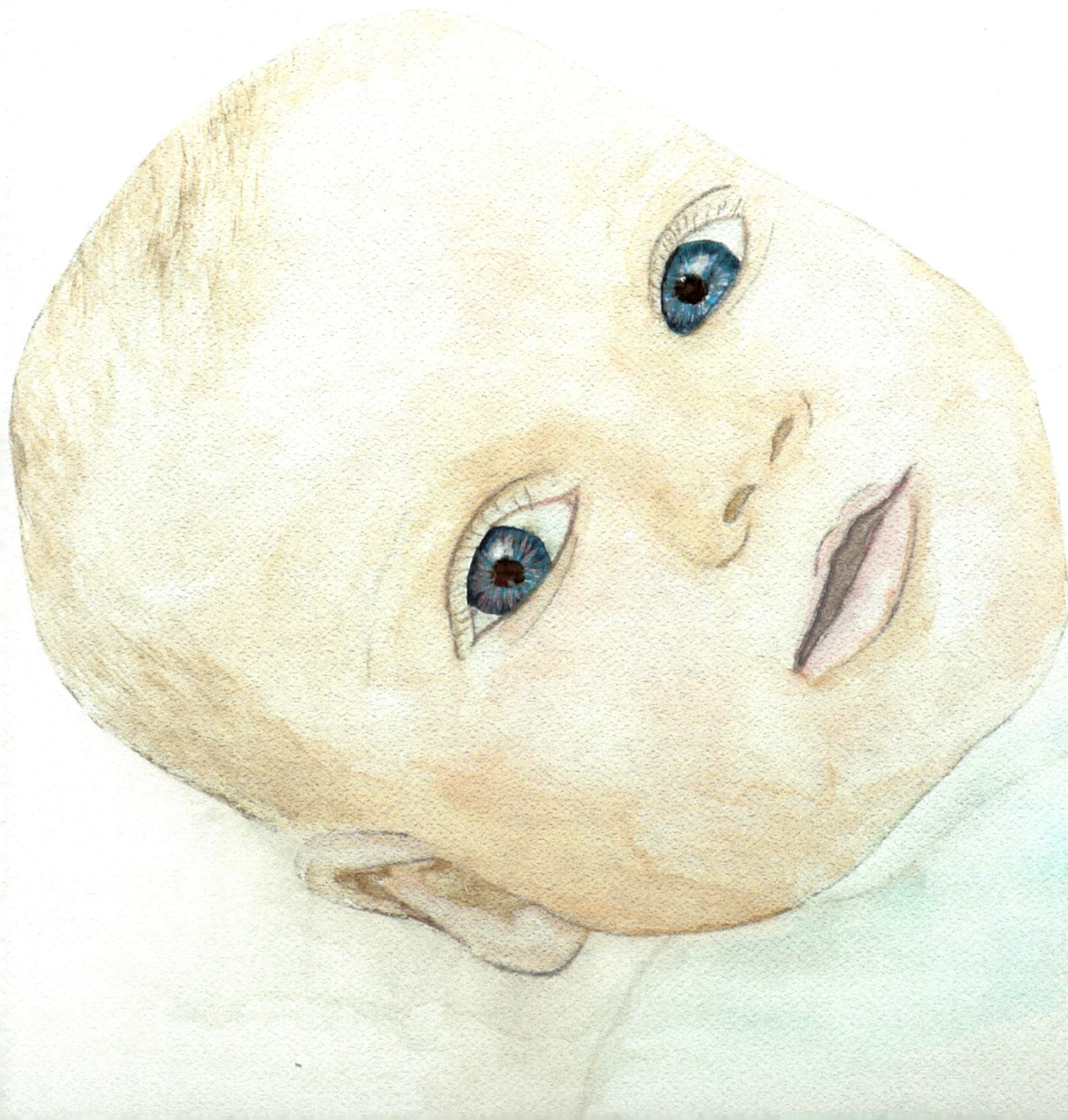

I think I recognize
that cute little grin.

I hold your soft hand
     and listen to your coo.

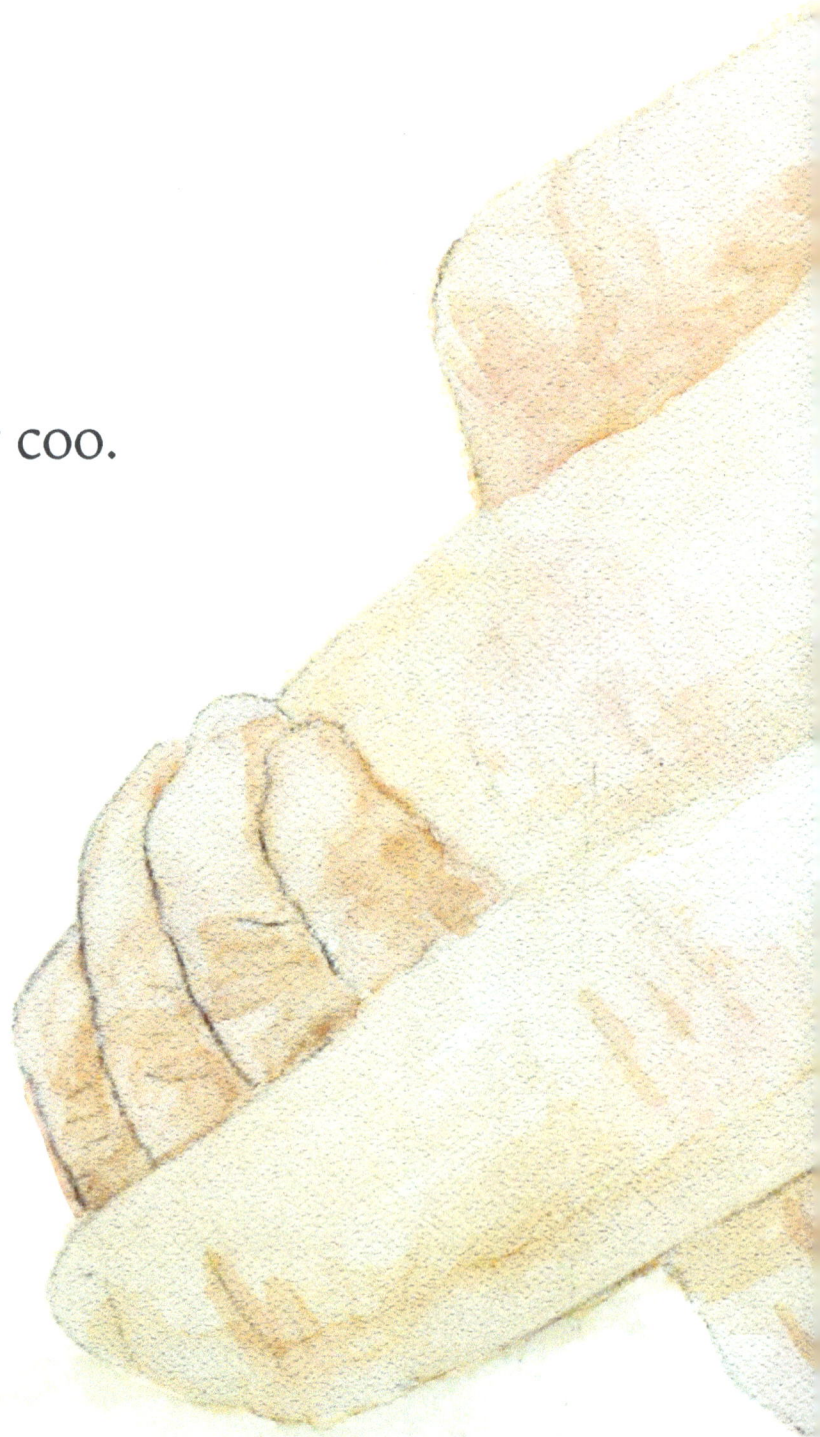

And I remember someone
a lot like you.

But you're new
and so special
and loved
quite a bit.

From your sweetly pursed lips
to your soft fingertips.

PEEKABOO!

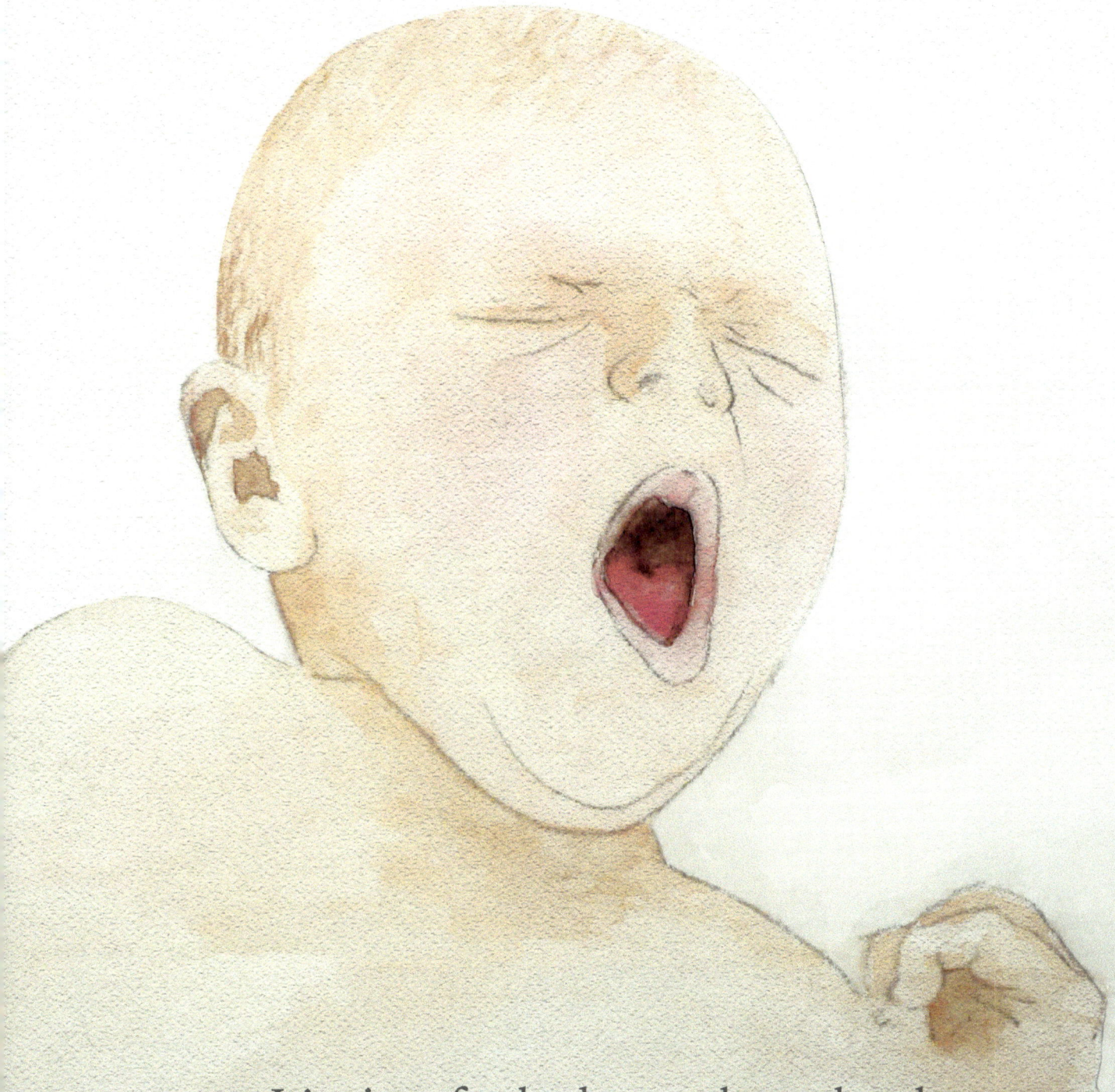

It's time for bed, you sleepy head.
We'll play again tomorrow.

But for now, I'll hold you
and remember the day

When I held someone special
the very same way.

For you're part of the future
that's formed from the past...

An echo, a reflection,
of love that will last.

I love you, Grandchild of Mine.

About the Author

After thirty years in a corporate setting, Elizabeth Reagan Milo is ready to tell stories that capture hearts and connect people. She's committed to children's literature as a means to create a love of learning, reinforce the importance of family, and introduce traditions that bring the generations together.
(And yes, she's a new Grandmother!)

About the Illustrator

With over twelve years in the design world, Kyzandrha Zarate has maintained a strong passion for fine art. Her original works have appeared in Jacksonville, Florida cafes, galleries and have won state awards. She prides herself in versatility and serving local residents and small businesses.